UNDERSTANDING INTERNET SECURITY

An easy to follow guide to keeping safe on-line

Austin Farrell

Webpage:

http://fazah19.wix.com/safetech

Facebook:

https://www.facebook.com/techocoach

Cover design by **Ted Chatain**

Copyright Austin Farrell 2014

Foreword

These days it is almost impossible to live a 'normal' life without using the Internet. We can get our news, buy shoes and keep in touch with our friends easily and quickly – but this magical system does have dangers for the unwary. We need to know about these dangers and make sure we protect ourselves.

In addition to our self-interest in protecting ourselves, we also have a collective responsibility to make sure our computers are not used to harm others.

This book is intended as a guide for the less expert Internet user who is keen to learn more about security, but is put off by all the jargon.

We look at what the main security threats are and some of the things we can do to make our on-line life safer.

Included also are explanations of what the terminology means plus some background on how we came to have our computers and the Internet.

CONTENTS

FOREWORD	3
INTRODUCTION	7
What is the Internet?	7
Why is the Internet insecure?	9
Why do we need to be concerned about Internet security?	11
What can we do to protect ourselves?	13
How is this book structured?	13
PART 1 – INTERNET BACKGROUND	**14**
Who thought of the Internet?	14
How does the Internet work?	16
How we connect to the Internet at home	19
What happens when the Internet messages leave our home?	22
Our Computers	24

PART 2 – THE INTERNET DANGERS AND WHAT TO DO ABOUT THEM   28

Who is causing the problem?   28

How do the bad guys get at us?   29

Technical Computer Attacks   30

Non-Technical Attacks   39

How can we protect our computers?   41

Some Rules for Internet Security   55

Some Rules for On-Line Shopping   57

More on Identity Theft   59

What do we do if we have an infection?   60

Useful On-Line Security Information   65

Suggested Security Routine   67

In Conclusion   69

PART 3: BUT WAIT, THERE'S MORE....   71

More about Bits, Bytes and Packets   72

How does anti-virus software work?   75

Security of Internet Transactions   77

What is VoIP?   88

What is Wi-Fi?   92

More on CERTs 95

Telecommunications 97

How did we end up with Personal Computers ?
109

How did the Internet happen? 119

Who Runs the Internet? 128

Digital Natives and Immigrants 130

The Psychology of Scams 136

Data Formats 146

'Staysmartonline' Factsheets 149

Introduction

What is the Internet?

A computer **network** is two or more computers connected so they can work together. Typical *'working together'* is exchanging messages or sharing a printer. Computers can be connected by cable or wireless, and these days most offices and many homes have a network.

The **Internet** is a vast world-wide collection of inter-connected computer networks. The Internet[1] uses a set of internationally agreed rules which allow all the different networks to work together.

The Internet is a bit like the roads system - it provides the infrastructure over which services are provided. The services we mostly use are **e-mail** and the **World Wide Web** (WWW).

The number of us using the Internet is now estimated to be approaching **2 billion**[2]- it is now so vast that it has been compared to the human brain in terms of complexity.

---

[1] **Always** spelt with a capital 'I'.

[2] Two thousand million.

Who uses the Internet?

Some countries use the Internet more than others. World Internet use might not be what you would expect – some examples (by language):

Language	Percentage
English	27%
Chinese	25%
Spanish	8%
Japanese	5%
German	4%
Russian	3%

Why is the Internet insecure?

When the Internet first started it was a small, closed system – the preserve of researchers and '*geeks*'[3]. Only trusted people were connected to it, so nobody needed to worry about security. None of the original designers anticipated the massive expansion of the Internet.

As the early Internet grew, mainly in US universities and research centres, the prevailing culture was open and cooperative. There were no commercial transactions to protect and identity theft was unheard of, so again security was not a high priority.

As the size and complexity of the Internet grew, it became harder and harder to anticipate all the security weaknesses, particularly in the software[4].

---

[3] Formerly a term of abuse, now used affectionately. The term is thought by some people to be derived from the early German word '*geck*', meaning a fool.

[4] If you read the disclaimers for the software on your computer, you will notice that the vendors don't accept responsibility for anything. This would not be acceptable for most other products or services.

Now that Internet commerce is huge, there is a big incentive for the unscrupulous to exploit the weaknesses in the system.

Great efforts have been made to improve Internet security, but it is a constant battle because of the cunning and persistence of criminals and recreational hackers.

Just as we need *'road sense'* to stay in one piece on the roads, we need *'Internet sense'* to survive on-line.

Why do we need to be concerned about Internet security?

When we use the Internet, we are all exposed.

There are tens of thousands of viruses[5] floating about the Internet, some of which could alter or delete our photos, documents and music or even physically damage our computer.

Skilled hackers[6] can exploit weakness in our computer software, or our own gullibility, to steal our cash and our identities - and they are extremely difficult to catch and prosecute.

If we engage in any transaction over the Internet which involves money - like Internet banking or buying things on e-bay, we are vulnerable to having our money stolen – possibly by people thousands of kilometres away who will never be charged with any offence.

---

[5] Viruses are discussed in detail later.

[6] We talk about the main hacker groups below.

Our identity could be stolen and used to open bank accounts or get identity documents in our name.

These threats (among many) are not academic or rare, but distinct possibilities if we do not take precautions.

While computer security might appear complicated, we do have a responsibility to ourselves to understand the pitfalls and do as much as we reasonably can to protect ourselves.

In the past five years, hackers are thought to be getting more skilled[7]. For example, Privacy Rights Clearinghouse[8] estimates that since 2005, **560 million** medical, financial and personal records have been stolen by hackers who have broken into government, hospital and company databases in the US.

Given this background, you would have to be stark, staring mad not to take precautions.

---

[7] According to **Robert Siciliano** of the McAfee anti-virus software company.

[8] Based in San Diego, California.

What can we do to protect ourselves?

Basically assume the worst and never underestimate the dangers.

We just need to learn and implement the basic security steps to security – like crossing the road, we need to look both ways every time.

The benefit will be peace of mind and possibly larger bank balances.

How is this book structured?

This book is divided into **three** parts:

- The first part gives a basic overview of how the Internet works;

- The second part discusses the main security threats and what we should do to deal with them; while

- The third part has more background about the development of computers and the Internet and some more detailed technical explanations.

Part 1 – Internet Background

Who thought of the Internet?[9]

The person who came up with the basic idea of the Internet was an American experimental psychologist, **J C R Licklider.**

While working with the military after the Second World War, Licklider recognised the power of computers to help researchers.

He later conceived the idea of interconnecting computers so researchers could easily exchange data and research papers. He wrote a memo to colleagues outlining his ideas, which he jokingly called the *'Galactic Network'*.

While a research leader with the US Defence Department's Advanced Research Projects Agency (DARPA), Licklider helped lay the technical foundations for what later became the Internet – there is more on this at the back of the book

---

[9] This could be a good trivial pursuit question.

J C R Licklider

The son of a Baptist minister, **Joseph Carl Robnett** Licklider was a tenured professor at MIT from 1968 to his retirement in 1985. At MIT he was very influential in developing time-shared computing.

Licklider, who was married with two daughters, was over 182 centimetres[10] tall and spoke with a Missouri accent. His hobby was restoring old cars.

He died of a heart attack (brought on by an asthma attack) in 1990. He was 75.

A question: Given the importance of the Internet, why have most people never heard of Licklider?

---

[10] Six feet in the archaic British Imperial measuring system.

How does the Internet work?

When you call on your mobile phone or landline, a **dedicated connection** is set up between your phone and the one you called. This connection is maintained for the duration of your call.

With the Internet, there are **no** dedicated connections. Messages (which may be anything - text, photos, videos) are sent as blocks of data (called '*packets*') in a series of steps. The Internet automatically works out the path the data packets should take.

In a sense, the Internet is more like the old telegraph system than the telephone because, for the most part, there is no **direct** connection between the sender and the receiver.

The technical rules which control how the Internet works are called '*protocols*'. These protocols are designed to allow all sorts of different systems (like PCs, Macs, tablets and mobile phones) to work smoothly together.

What do we mean when we say 'digital'?

The first electrical communication system was the telegraph, which revolutionised the 19th century world. Suddenly, news from distant parts zipped over the wires in hours rather than weeks or even months.

Telegraph operators tapped out messages in a simple code - 'Morse Code' - named after **Samuel Morse**, a telegraph pioneer (Sam as a young man on the right).

Morse Code uses combinations of a 'dot' or a 'dash' – for example, the distress message SOS (standing for "Save Our Souls") is represented by '. . . _ _ _ . . .'

In the digital world, messages and data are also stored and transmitted in a code, but this time the code uses two **digits** - a **0** (zero) or a **1** (one).

Everything – text, data, pictures, voice, maps, music, video – is represented by strings of zeroes and ones. There are international standards for coding all these things – all we have to know is which standard is being used.

The basic element for data storage in a computer[11] is either a 0 or a 1 – called a **'bit'**. The numbering system using these two digits is called the **binary** system.

By convention, bits are generally stored in groups of eight bits called a **'byte'**.[12]

As an example, any letter of the alphabet can be represented by the first seven bits of a byte, while the eighth bit is a check bit (called a *'parity'* bit), included to detect errors in transmission or storage. So in very rough terms, a byte is equivalent to one letter.

There is more on this later – see *'More on bits and bytes'*.

---

[11] Computers in this book generally include PCs, Apples, laptops, Smartphones and Tablets.

[12] A standard way of giving the size of computer memory is in **'megabytes'**, where a megabyte is one million bytes.

How we connect to the Internet at home

Internet users in large business and government connect directly to the digital world. Their Internet traffic goes straight in and out as a digital data stream. The same goes for Smartphone[13] users.

Most home and small business users are different. Until a real national broadband service is rolled out to homes in Australia[14], for most of us the landline phone connection is still the same as it was in the 19th century - **analogue**. This means that the signals between our homes and our local telephone exchange are in the form of voltage variations which follow the loudness and pitch of our voices.

Because computers are digital, we need a device to convert the computer's digital signals to analogue form. That device is a **modem**.

---

[13] Smartphones are mobile phones with the capabilities of a small, handheld computer. They usually have a relatively large screen and use an operating system (like 'Android') to manage the phone's operation.

[14] Which may or may not be in our lifetime.

Modems (short for **mod**ulator/**dem**odulator) were originally developed for fax machines. In a fax, modems convert the black letter information (on white pages) into sound tones (the '*modulator*' part). The tones are sent along the telephone lines to the local exchange where they are converted into digital form and sent off to their destination.

To receive a fax the process is reversed - the sound tones coming from your local exchange are converted back into black letter information (the '*demodulator*' part) and printed on white paper.

The fax modems were later modified for use with computers.

There are basically two sorts of modem:

- Older *'dial-up'* modems which can run up to about **56 kilobytes** (56,000 bytes) per second; and
- ADSL[15] modems, which can run up to about **8 megabytes** (8 million bytes) per second.

Most people in Australia can now be connected by ADSL modem in their home or small business.

The speed of ADSL modems depends on how far we are from our local exchange – the farther we are from the exchange, the slower it gets[16].

Our ADSL connections require a special unit at the exchange end (excitingly known as a DSLAM)[17]. Most, but not all, telephone exchanges are equipped with DSLAMs.

---

[15] ADSL stands for **'Asymmetric Digital Serial Line'** – they are arranged to download data **to** our computers far faster than they can upload data **from** our computers.

[16] With an optic fibre Internet connection, there is no slowing with distance. This is covered in more detail later.

[17] DSLAM stands for **'Digital Serial Line Access Module'**.

What happens when the Internet messages leave our home?

Your computer divides up each message you send (say an e-mail) into series of data blocks called '*packets*'. Each packet has a section up the front which (among other things) contains the destination address, the packet size and the packet sequence number (in case the packets arrive in the wrong order).

The packets are sent firstly to your local exchange and then on to your Internet Service Provider (ISP). From the ISP, the packets thread their way across the Internet universe to their destination computer where they are assembled in the correct order.

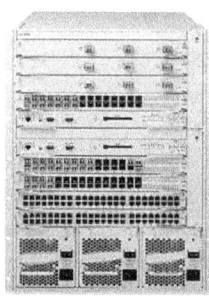

The packets travel in a series of 'hops' along the way from one **router** to the next.

Routers (like the one on the left) are electronic machines which look at the packet headers, decide where they should go next and send them on their way – a bit like mail sorters.

How do the routers know where to send the packets? The Internet has a wonderful automatic '*phone book*' called the **Domain Name System** (DNS). The DNS is arranged as a hierarchy of '***domain**s*', with the top layer being the country – for example, you will know that Australia is the '.au' domain.

The next layer is the functional area – examples being the '.gov' (for all three layers of government), '.edu' for schools and universities and '.com' for businesses.

The final layer is the institution or business itself – for example, the Australian Bureau of Meteorology is '.bom'.

If you send an e-mail to someone in the Australian Bureau of Meteorology, the address might be something like:

> joe.blow@bom.gov.au

The DNS system provides the information for the routers to direct the e-mail packets along the path to the 'bom.gov.au' mail server[18], where it is re-directed to Joe Blow's terminal.

---

[18] A server is just a computer with special software dedicated to a particuler task – for instance a mail server deals with e-mail.

When you look for a web page, your computer sends a request message to the web server (which could be, say, www.bom.gov.au). The request message contains the address of the web server, the specific page requested (usually the '*Home*' page), and the return address (your computer).

Our Computers

This is mainly about PCs, but it mostly applies to laptops, Apples, Smartphones and Tablet computers (like iPads).

Computers can be looked at from two angles – **hardware** and **software**.

The hardware refers to the computer box and what are usually called the *'peripherals'* - the keyboard, the mouse, the screen, the printer, a camera and so on.

The real problems from the security point of view reside in the software – the set of instructions which make the whole thing useful.

Computers have at least **three** sorts of software:

The most important is the **operating system**, a program which orchestrates the operation of the computer. Most computers (more than 90%) have a Microsoft operating system (like '8', '7' or 'Vista'), Apple computers (about 5%) have their own Apple 'OS' operating system, while a very small number of computers use

'Linux'[19]. Quite a few Smartphones use Google 'Android'.

A second type of software, which is completely invisible to users, is a **driver**. These small software packages connect the operating system to the peripherals (like the printer, the mouse, webcams and so on) – each peripheral has its own special driver software.

And finally, we have the **applications**[20] which allow us to do useful things like sending e-mails, creating document and searching the web. Most computers use Microsoft Office application software.

From the security point of view, most of the software vulnerabilities are in the common applications and operating systems.

Why is this so? The basic reason is that computer software has grown in size and complexity. Some of the larger operating systems have tens of millions of lines in the source code. Most of us will never use all the bells and whistles in the software, but vendors insist on including them.

---

[19] Linux is free, but for most people it is not as easy to use as a Microsoft operating systems.

[20] Referred to as '*Apps*' on Tablets and Smartphones.

The downside of this growing size and complexity is that it leads to coding errors and unforeseen vulnerabilities in the software. Hackers are constantly trying to find these vulnerabilities to exploit.

The more common the operating system and applications are, the more likely hackers are to attack them – hackers follow market share.

When they become aware of a problem, the software vendors quickly devise patches[21] to fix the vulnerability and make these patches available free to their customers.

The process of downloading and inserting the patches can be entirely automatic, provided you set up your computer to do this.

UPDATES

For your security, it is **vital** that all software updates and patches are installed as soon as they are available.

---

[21] The patches to fix problems are generally referred to as *'updates'* by the software companies.

Part 2 – The Internet Dangers and what to do about them

Who is causing the problem?

There are lots of bad people in the Internet world, but main problem groups are:

- **Criminal hackers** who steal identities and credit card numbers either for their own use or to be sold on to other criminals. They may also operate scams using fake websites or send out dodgy offers or investment schemes;

- **Recreational hackers** who get a kick out of finding and exploiting flaws in our software. They often don't steal anything, but can cause major disruption to the Internet; damage to computer software and loss of data; and

- **Protest hackers** who have an axe to grind. One tactic they sometimes use is a *'Denial of Service'* attack (discussed later).

Although they will generally not trouble home or small business users, **government hackers** are thought to be quietly preparing for future '*Cyber Wars*'.

Cyber Warfare

The theory is that military hackers will steal classified information or disable enemy infrastructure using the Internet.

The world's first military '*cyberweapon*', '***Stuxnet***', was alleged to have been used by the United States and Israel against Iranian nuclear facilities[22].

How do the bad guys get at us?

The bad guys have two basic approaches:

- Gaining access to our computers, tablets and smartphones by exploiting **software weaknesses**; and

- Tricking us into giving our vital information or money using various scams, fake e-mails and fake websites.

---

[22] According to the on-line newsletter '*Crypto-Gram*', 12-Nov-2012.

Let's look at the software approach first:

Technical Computer Attacks

Software programs which can do our computer harm are generally know as **malware** (from **mal**icious/soft**ware**). A typical way to get into our computer is for a bad guy to send us an e-mail with a malware attachment. We open the attachment and – bingo, we are infected.

Another way is through infected web sites, particularly the less common or oddball ones.

Clever malware hides itself in odd places in the computer so that it is very hard to find. The malware is generally sent in the form of an '*executable*' – a program which starts running on the computer and does something bad.

The various types of malware have been given names which suggest how they work – names like '*virus*', '*worm*' and '*Trojan*', but the distinctions between these names is often blurred.

Viruses

Real viruses can't live for long outside an animal or human host and they use the host's cells to reproduce. Computer viruses can reproduce themselves in computers, but need a means of some kind to move across the Internet to other computers – means usually referred to as a '*vectors*', following the medical terminology.

A typical virus might arrive in your computer attached to an e-mail. After hiding itself, the virus might be programmed to look through your e-mail address list and send a copy of itself to everyone on that list.

Computer viruses can be programmed to do a wide variety of things to your computer, some benign and some destructive. Some of the more vicious viruses destroy files and in some cases even destroy the hard disk.

Worms

Typical worms reproduce themselves and spread from computer to computer in much the same way as viruses. However, they generally don't damage the infected computers. Their main effect is to clog up the links between the infected computers, slowing everything down.

THE MORRIS WORM

The first major malware was the 'Morris Worm', created by **Robert Morris**, a Cornell University student.

The worm was particularly embarrassing for the lad's Dad who worked for the agency tasked (among other things) with protecting US government computers[23].

Morris released the worm in November 1988 from the Massachusetts Institute of Technology (MIT) in an attempt to cover his tracks. Estimates of the number of computers infected vary, but some seem to think it was about 10% of the 60,000 computers then connected to the Internet.

Despite his efforts to hide, Morris was tracked down, charged under the 1986 US *Computer Fraud and Abuse Act* and found guilty. He was sentenced in March 1991 to three-years probation, 400 hours of community service and a $US10,000 fine.

Morris is now a Professor at MIT and a partner in the 'Y Combinator' company.

---

[23] The US **National Security Agency** (NSA).

Trojans

A Trojan is a term for malware which is disguised as something attractive or useful, but is in reality harmful and allows a hacker to attack or control your computer. The term relates to the Ancient Greek tale (see below).

A Trojan may be a program which records what you type on your keyboard[24] (like passwords) and sends the results to a hacker.

It could even be a program which allows the hacker to take complete control of your PC, as if he or she was sitting at your keyboard.

---

[24] Sometimes referred to as a '*keyboard logger*'.

TROJAN

The term 'Trojan' refers to a story from the Trojan War in Greek mythology.

Excavations near **Hissarlik**, on the west coast of Turkey, suggest that there may be some truth in the story of the siege and destruction of the city of Troy by Greek forces - perhaps in the Bronze Age sometime around 1190 BC.

The story goes that the Greek forces besieging Troy built a very large wooden horse (the horse being the symbol of Troy) and left it as a gift in front of the city before pretending to leave. The defenders of Troy brought the wooden horse inside the city gates.

At night, Greek soldiers hidden inside the horse crept out and opened the city gates, letting the attackers in.

A *'Trojan Horse'* is thus synonymous with something which looks innocent, but is actually very dangerous.

Spyware

Spyware is a general term for malware inserted into your computer (without your permission or knowledge) which gathers information (like passwords and credit card details) and sends it to a hacker. Spyware can arrive by a variety of routes – for instance it may be hidden in free software or even music.

Identity theft

Spyware is one of the ways in which hackers gather information about you. They may then use this information to pretend to be you and get identity cards or set up bank accounts in your name. Some people have had their lives ruined by identity theft.

Denial of Service Attacks

A very elaborate form of computer attack is the so-called *'Denial of Service'*(DoS) attack. While there are many variations of the scheme, the basics remain the same.

With the owners being completely unaware of it, an attacker infects a large number of computers[25] with special software.

---

[25] It could be tens of thousands.

The infected computers are known as *'zombies'* or *'bots'* (from ro**bots**) and the entire collection of infected computers is often referred to as a *'zombie army'* or *'botnet'* (ro**bot net**work).

On command from the attacker, all the infected computers simultaneously send requests to a target (for instance a bank's website) and completely overwhelm its capacity – effectively shutting it down.

This sort of thing can be used by hackers with a political axe to grind or those seeking a ransom payment from the target.

While you are not directly responsible for the attack if your computer is infected, your Internet access can be blocked by authorities until the infection is removed.

Data Ransoming

Some businesses (including medical practices) have been the subject of ransom attacks. Their computers have been infiltrated and their files encrypted (that is, scrambled and rendered unreadable). The attackers then demand a ransom for providing the key to unlock the files[26].

While this is a rare occurrence, it can make life extremely difficult for a small to medium business with inadequate backup[27].

---

[26] With the ransom demand often being relatively small (maybe a few hundred dollars), the embarrassed victims pay up and don't report the attack.

[27] As an example, a medical practice on the Queensland Gold Coast was subject to a ransom attack in 2013.

Non-Technical Attacks

'Social Engineering'

Conning us to give access to our computers or divulge personal information is sometimes referred to as *'social engineering'*. Some of the greatest hackers were not great on the technical side, but were absolutely brilliant at gaining access to computers through phone calls or masquerading as delivery men.

Never respond to a phone call or an e-mail asking for your computer user identification ('UserID') or password.

Phishing

Phishing is a term for information gathering (usually for passwords or credit card details) using fake requests.

It may take the form of a fake e-mail request, apparently from your bank, saying that you need to send your User ID and password to verify your account after a computer malfunction.

Most of these attempts fail, but a small percentage is successful and make it worth the scammers while.

Scams

There are many types of Internet scams, including:

- E-mails asking to use your bank account to deposit a large sum of money;

- Notification of a lottery win (which you didn't know you had entered) asking for your bank details to deposit the winnings; and

- Fake websites, some of which will come up if you make a small error typing in the website name

---

Fake Websites

Scammers register fake websites looking just like the real thing, but with a slightly different website address.

The website address[28] (which appears near the top left of your browser) should be checked carefully before any financial transaction.

---

[28] Sometimes referred to as a URL (**Universal Resource Locator**).

How can we protect our computers?

Internet security involves continuous vigilance and attention to detail. It is often tedious, but the end result justifies your efforts.

The basic approach to Internet security is not to rely on one thing, but to create a **series of barriers** to make life as difficult as possible for potential attackers.

Anti-Virus Software

Your most important safeguard is up-to-date anti-virus software loaded at all times. This should be the very first thing you do and preferably before you connect to the Internet.

Anti-virus software works by looking for the '*signature*' of all **known** malware in the incoming traffic.

ANTI-VIRUS SOFTWARE

Installing anti-virus software and automatically updating it every day is the single most important security measure for your computer.

Many operating systems (like 'Vista', '7' and '8') have a basic anti-virus software component, but many users consider it prudent to have anti-virus software from a specialist company which automatically updates the software every day.

There are over 200 offerings in the security software market. To help us choose, computer magazines (like '*PC Magazine*') publish annual reviews of security software, with rankings of performance and price. Prominent vendors include AVG, McAfee, Norton and Kaspersky.

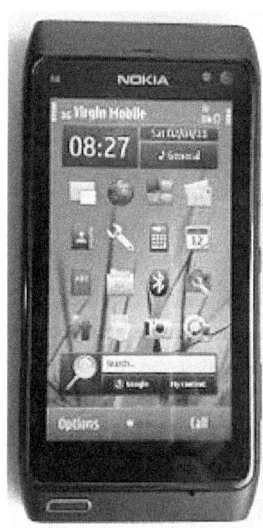

Some companies provide free anti-virus software for home users – for instance **Microsoft Security Essentials** for Microsoft users – but most charge an annual fee of the order of $70 to $100 or so. Look for specials which can reduce the cost quite a bit.

Free anti-virus software for home users can be downloaded from:

- **Antivir** (*http://www.freeav.com/*);

- **Avast** (*http://www.avast.com/*);

- **AVG** (*http://www.avg.com/product-avg-anti-virus-free-edition*); and

- **ClamWin** (*http://www.clamwin.com/content/view/18/46/*)

A free malware scanner is available from Malwarebytes.org. This combs through your computer looking for viruses. The full version (Malwarebytes PRO, cost about $25) also identifies and blocks access to infected websites.

There is more on how anti-virus software operates later in the book.

Firewalls

Firewalls are software programs designed to monitor and control what goes in and out of your computer. More specifically they are used to alert you to unusual or potentially harmful activity within your computer or in traffic coming into or going out of your computer.

Firewalls work in concert with anti-virus software – the anti-virus software tries to prevent the bad stuff entering or staying in our computers while firewalls generally look for the **effects** of the bad stuff. Most firewalls will halt a suspect activity and tell you about it. You then make the decision to allow or disallow that activity.

An example could be attempts by your computer to contact a website without your specific command – which may indicate the presence of malware, but it could be a routine software updating activity.

Firewall software can be sold together with anti-virus software or it can be sold separately.

For home users, Zonealarm[29] provides a free firewall.

---

[29] Google '*Zonealarm Free Firewall*'.

Browser Security

Your browser is a software application which allows you to look at websites. Browsers have their own security setting which you can adjust to suit your needs.

The higher you set your security levels, the fewer website features you will have available, but the more secure your browser will be. You have to decide on the right balance for you. If in doubt, set the security level to *'high'*.

The details of how to set your browser security settings depend on the browser you are using.

For the most common browser setting information, try:

Microsoft Internet Explorer:

http://windows.microsoft.com/en-AU/internet-explorer/ie-security-privacy-settings#ie=ie-11

Mozilla Firefox

https://support.mozilla.org/en-US/products/firefox/privacy-and-security

Google Chrome

https://support.google.com/chrome/answer/95572?hl=en

Apple Safari

http://support.apple.com/kb/ht1677

Opera

http://www.opera.com/help/tutorials/security/control/

As with all your software, make sure you install your browser updates as soon as they become available.

Check for Browser Plug-In Updates

To work well, your browser (such as Microsoft Explorer, Google Chrome and Modzilla Firefox) generally loads additional software – referred to '*plug-ins'*.

Typical plug-ins are Adobe Flash Player and Shockwave Player. These programs allow you to see all the website bells and whistles.

When your browser software is updated, your plug-ins may not be automatically updated at the same time. You can use a plug-in checker (such as the free Qualys BrowserCheck), which not only checks for non-updated plug-ins, but also allows you to load the updates.

This is to stop hackers attacking your computer through non-updated plug-ins.

Anti-Phishing Procedures

While not always completely effective, we can use two complimentary approaches to combat phishing attacks.

The first step is to configure our e-mail software to warn us of suspect e-mails.

The configuration procedures are covered in:

Factsheet 4 (for Microsoft Outlook Express);

Factsheet 5 (for Mozilla Thunderbird); and

Factsheet 7 (for Microsoft Live Mail)

on the Staysmartonline website[30].

The second step is to turn on the anti-phishing feature in your web browser (in case you inadvertently click on a phishing website link in an e-mail).

This is usually done by clicking on the '*Tools*' tab and selecting the anti-phishing feature on the security menu.

ADSL Modem and Wireless Router Security

Many Internet Service Providers (ISPs) supply a combined ADSL Modem and Wireless Router in a single box as part of your deal.

The box usually incorporates a firewall and a number of security features which are the default settings, but it is a good idea to check what you have been given.

---

[30]*http://www.staysmartonline.gov.au/factsheets*

The ISP may supply the instructions to check or set up the security on the box. If not, good tutorials on the procedures to check are contained in:

> **Factsheet 16** *'Securely configuring your broadband modem/router';* and
>
> **Factsheet 17** *'Wireless (Wi-Fi) Security'*[31]

If you have an ADSL or other broadband connection, you are directly exposed to the Internet outside world (and potential attacks). To reduce your exposure, it is a good idea to switch off your computer (or Tablet or Smartphone) when you are not using it.

---

[31] Both available from *http://www.staysmartonline.gov.au/factsheets*

Passwords

A lot of security is based on *'two factor authentication'*. An example would be your ATM[32] cash card, where the card itself is one *'factor'* and your PIN code (known only to you and very difficult to guess) is the other.

If an incorrect PIN code is put in three times in succession, most ATM or credit cards will be disabled as a security measure.

Logging in to your Internet account is very similar – you have your user identification (ID), like *'joe.blow'*, and a secret password chosen by you.

Since your user ID is often the same as the first part of your e-mail address, it is important that your password is strong.

What does a '**strong**' password mean?

Computer hackers sometimes use a '***dictionary attack***' to guess your password. They drop malware into your computer which tries every word in the dictionary. They may also try every birthday date or common pet's names. This sort of thing can be done automatically in seconds.

---

[32] Automatic Teller Machine

To combat this, passwords should never be a dictionary word and should be a mixture upper and lower case letters with at least one number or symbol.

An example would be '**P@ny+Clu6**'.

The longer and more mixed the password is, the 'stronger' it is, meaning it is harder to guess. Ideally, your passwords should be at least **eight** characters long. Some banks have specific requirements for length and content.

If we write down our passwords, make sure we keep them in a secure place that nobody else knows about - since we should never share our passwords with anyone else

Having different passwords for different applications is a good idea, as is regularly changing your password (ideally twice a year) – just in case someone has worked out what yours is.

Adam Levin[33] recommends **not** clicking the '*Save Password*' button when using your Smartphone. If you lose your phone, it makes it much easier for the thief to access your data and identity.

---

[33] Founder of the US firm '*Identity Theft 911*'.

Backing Up

Since computers occasionally collapse in a heap, it is a good idea to regularly save ('back up') your vital data on a CD, DVD, USB stick or an external hard drive.

Most operating systems (like Vista, '7', and '8') have a utility part which allows you to back up your data regularly.

The Australian Department of Communications has an excellent Factsheet[34] with instructions on how to do this.

As an alternative to your own storage devices, Zonealarm offer a free data backup service of up to **5 Gigabytes** over the Internet. You can set this service to do a backup every day.

Printing out your e-mail address book from time to time is also useful because recovering your e-mail stuff can be complicated.

---

[34] ***Factsheet 12**–'How to create back-up copies of your important information'* - at
http://www.staysmartonline.gov.au/factsheets.

Cloud computing

Cloud computing is gathering pace in the business sector and is starting to become more common in homes, so what exactly is it?

PCs, laptops and Mac computers have large amounts of data storage available on **hard disc drives** (HDD).

Hard Disc Drives

Hard discs are metal, ceramic or glass discs spinning very fast (typically about **6,000** revolutions per minute).

Our data is recorded on a very thin layer of magnetic material deposited on the disc surface. We get extra storage space by stacking several disks on a spindle.

Data is recorded or read by moving read/write 'heads' which float just above the spinning discs on a thin layer of air.

Once recorded, the data can last for years, and we can read it as many times as we like without affecting it. However, we can re-use the disc space by recording something else in place of the existing data.

To reduce size and cost, mobile computing devices like Smartphones and Tablets do **not** have hard discs and cannot store a lot of data.

We get around this by sending our data over the Internet to servers in large data centres (the '*Cloud*') – we don't need to know where these servers are. Our data is password protected and generally encrypted[35] so no one else can read it.

When we need your data, we download it from the Cloud – provided we have Internet access.

Free Clouds

Some companies offer free cloud storage. For example, Yahoo have a photo storage service called '*Flickr*' offering **1 Terabyte** (one million megabytes) of free cloud storage. This can store about **600,000 photos**.

Google also offers a similar (but smaller) free cloud service for Smartphones and Tablets.

Apple iPad and iPhone users get a free iCloud service (and get extra storage space for a fee).

---

[35] Encrypted means the data is scrambled so that it cannot be understood by anyone else. There is more on encryption later.

Some Rules for Internet Security

- **Never** connect your computing device (PC, laptop, Tablet, Smartphone) to the Internet without anti-virus software and preferably a firewall[36];

- Make sure that your anti-virus and firewall profiles are **automatically updated** regularly, preferably every day;

- **Ensure** that operating system and application software **updates** are downloaded and installed automatically or as soon as possible;

- Run a complete **manual security scan** of your computer about once a week;

- Be **very careful** opening e-mails from people you don't know and **do not** open an e-mail attachment from someone you don't know or trust;

- Check the security settings on your browser;

- Be wary of accessing websites that seem a little odd;

---

[36] Or make it the very first thing you do on the Internet.

- Check that you have typed in the correct web address when you open a website;

- Use '**strong**' passwords and change them regularly;

- **Don't** tell anyone your passwords (or put it on a yellow post-it note under your keyboard) and **never** provide User ID or passwords to anyone over the phone or Internet;

- Turn off your computing device when you are not using it; and

- Consider minimising your personal details in the social media (Facebook, etc.).

Some Rules for On-Line Shopping

Suggested tips for improving your on-line shopping security are:

- Avoid odd-looking websites (spelling mistakes, things out of alignment, those that have a funny feel about them, etc.);

- Check the address of the website (the stuff like '*www.bom.gov.au*' at the top of the browser) to make sure it is what you intended;

- Before you hit the '*Buy*' button, read the product description carefully and make sure it is what you want - including postage and handling and other charges and the refund and complaints policies;

- Bargains which look too good to be true often are;

- Only pay using a secure web page (one that uses the term 'SSL' and has a padlock symbol)[37];

---

[37] SSL (Secure Socket Layer) is discussed a little later.

- **Always** use a secure payment method such as PayPal, BPay, or your credit card. **Do not** use money transfers and direct debit, and never send your bank or credit card details by email;

- **Always** print and keep a copy of the receipt and keep all emails to and from the seller; and

- If using an auction site (like e-Bay or Graysonline) always conduct transactions within the auction website. **Do not** deal directly with the seller (even if they offer a better deal).

More on Identity Theft

While most identity theft occurs via the Internet, some is due to bad people snooping around your house.

Suggestions to minimise the risk include:

- Before throwing them out, shred all documents with bank account numbers and similar details;

- Put a padlock on your letterbox;

- If an expected bill does not arrive by post, check to see why (it may have been stolen);

- Set up an SMS (mobile phone) notification with your financial institution for larger transactions; and

- Check all your bank and credit card statements in detail (even banks make mistakes).

What do we do if we have an infection?

You have installed anti-virus software and a firewall, and you have been very careful opening e-mail attachments and avoiding odd websites. Despite all this, something bad has got through.

Sometimes the signs of infection are clear – things have gone horribly wrong - but sometimes the signs are not so obvious.

Some signs

Many viruses and Trojans are designed to be stealthy, so by their very nature they are hard to notice. Some things to look for include:

- Your computer suddenly changes behaviour in some way, for example, it is more sluggish or slow to respond to commands;

- A sudden outbreak of unexplained 'crashes'; or

- Odd messages in your outgoing mail or sent folder which you cannot recall sending.

If you see these or similar signs, **don't ignore them – do something.** You may need to ask a more experienced user to help.

What can we try?

Step 1[38]

[**Note**: If your computer will not boot (start), go straight to **Step 4** below.]

Update your installed anti-virus software, then run a full system manual anti-virus scan. This may take some time.

When the full scan is completed, check the '*detected problems*[39]' window and delete any detected malware.

Re-start your computer and see if this has made any difference.

Bear in mind that sophisticated malware is designed to avoid detection by virus scanning software. Sometimes, if one brand fails, another will succeed.

---

[38] The suggestions in this section are largely based on **Factsheet 11, Parts 1, 2 and 3** on the Staysmartonline website.

[39] Each anti-virus package will use a different term.

Step 2

If your first try does not succeed, try a post-infection tool from another vendor.
For example, download, update and run Malwarebytes[40] (which is compatible with most anti-virus packages).

Delete any detected malware, restart your computer and see if this makes a difference.

Step 3

If no progress has been made, try a web-based tool. Free examples include:

- **BitDefender**
  (*http://www.bitdefender.com/scan8/ie.html;*)

- **ESET**
  (*http://www.eset.com/onlinescan/*);

- **F-Secure**
  (*http://support.fsecure.com/enu/home/ols.shtml*);

- **Microsoft**
  (*http://onecare.live.com/site/enus/center/howsafe.htm*);

---

[40] From http://www.malwarebytes.org

- **McAfee**
  (http://us.mcafee.com/root/mfs/default.asp); and

- **Trend-Micro**
  (http://housecall.trendmicro.com/)

[**Note:** Do **not** use a web-based tool from the same vendor as your installed anti-virus software. Note also that you need '*Administrator*' privileges to run these tools.]

Run the tool and delete any detected malware.

When finished, restart your computer and see if this makes any difference.

Step 4

If the first three steps don't work, or if your computer won't start, it is probably time to make and run a so-called '***bootable disc***'. You may need some assistance with this step.

To make a 'bootable disc', you need to find another (working) computer connected to the Internet and have an unused CD ready.

The steps, which are quite complicated, are described in detail in **Factsheet 11, Part 3** on the Staysmartonline website[41].

If this process fails, you may have to call in a professional.

---

[41] *http://www.staysmartonline.gov.au/factsheets*

Useful On-Line Security Information

The most useful on-line source of security information for Australian home and small business users is the Department of Communications '**Staysmartonline**' website:

    http://www.staysmartonline.gov.au/

This site contains a very well presented set of tips and instructions, with a particularly helpful set of 'Factsheets' at:

http://www.staysmartonline.gov.au/factsheets

While some of the Factsheets (the list is at the end of the book) are a little dated, many have step-by-step instructions which walk the user through complicated things like security settings.

A more general security reference website is at the Australian Government portal:

    http://australia.gov.au/topics/it-and-communications/cyber-security

If you are really into information security and are having trouble sleeping, a good cure is the 313-page *'Australian Government Information Security Manual'*, available at:

www.asd.gov.au/publications/Information_Security_Manual_2010.pdf

Suggested Security Routine

Initial (with a new computer):

Before connecting to the Internet:

- Set all computer security setting (select 'Settings')
- Set your installed browser security settings;
- Check the ADSL modem and WiFi security settings (and note the WiFi access code);
- Set 'automatic updates' for all installed applications software (eg Microsoft Office);
- Get, install and set 'automatic updates' for:
  - Anti-Virus software;
  - Firewall; and a
  - Malware scanner.

Connect to the Internet and update the profiles for the:

- Anti-Virus software; and
- Firewall;

Annual

Get, install and update the new annual version of:

- Anti-Virus software;
- Firewall; and your
- Malware scanner.

Weekly

- Run a full manual malware scan of your computer and remove any unwanted malware or 'cookies';
- Back up all important files (on an external drive, USB drive, CD or DVD) and store the result in another (preferably fireproof) location;

Daily

- Make sure all operating system and application software updates are installed;
- Delete without opening all suspicious e-mails; and
- Back up any really important files (or photos or music);
- Turn off computer, modem, router and Wi-Fi when not in use.

In Conclusion

"The condition upon which God hath given liberty to man[42] is eternal vigilance."

John Philpot Curran[43] (Irish Politician & Judge)

It is impossible to guarantee complete security on the Internet, but we can make life a good deal safer for ourselves by developing a *'culture of security'* – a series of strategies and habits that make things as difficult as possible for the bad guys. Make your own good luck by trying the following:

Defend in Depth: Don't rely on one thing. Set all your security levels (eg on your modem/router, operating system, browser, applications, etc.) to the highest levels you can live with;

---

[42] I'm sure John meant women as well.

[43] From County Cork, John overcame a bad stutter by reading literature in front of a mirror and survived at least five pistol duels. He founded a drinking club in Dublin known as *'The Order of St Patrick'*. His original 1790 phrase is sometimes paraphrased as *'The price of liberty is eternal vigilance'* and attributed to lesser mortals.

Develop a Routine: Make sure all your software is updated as regularly as possible. Reward yourself with a chocolate frog when you do your security routine;

Be Paranoid: Look with suspicion at everything coming in to your computer – if in doubt, delete. Check any unusual behaviour as soon as possible;

Have a Fall-back Position: If it all goes pear-shaped, your daily or weekly back-up is where you move forward from; and

Keep Learning: Read. Talk to knowledgeable relatives and friends. In the computer and Internet world no one knows everything, and even if you knew everything today, it would be different tomorrow (or even later today). The only constant is change[44].

---

[44] A saying generally attributed to **Heraclitus of Ephesus** (535 BC – 475 BC)

Part 3: But wait, there's more....

More about Bits, Bytes and Packets

We usually use ten numbers to count – 1 to 9 plus the 0. We count up to 9, then carry on the 10 – the **decimal** system.

Fibonacci

The decimal system (also known as the Hindu-Arabic system of numbers) was introduced to Europe in 1202 by **Leonardo Pisano Bigollo** (better known as *'Fibonacci'*) in his book *'Liber Abaci'* (*Book of Calculations*)[45].

Fibonacci was the son of Guglielmo Bonacci, a wealthy merchant from Pisa, Italy, who operated a trading post in what is now Algeria.

While travelling with his Dad in North Africa, Leon learned about the decimal system, which he realised was far simpler that the cumbersome Roman system in use in Europe at the time.

Regarded as one of the best mathematicians of his age, Leon died aged 80 in 1250.

---

[45] You can see a beautiful handwritten copy in the National Library in Florence.

But there are other ways of counting, however bizarre they may sound. Computers count with two numbers only – 1 and 0. With this system we count up to 1 and then carry on the 0 – the **binary** system. A binary digit (shortened to 'bit') is the basic information element.

Computers store all information in binary code – all the computer needs to know is what format is being used.

As an example, computers often encode the alphabet using ASCII[46]. This is what it looks like:

Letter	Binary Code
A	0001
B	0010
C	0011
D	0100
E	0101
F	0110
G	0111
H	1000
I	1001

and so on.

---

[46] Originating in 1962, ASCII is thought to be the first computer standard. ASCII stands for **American Standard Code for Information Interchange.**

Because all letters (upper and lower case), decimal digits and punctuation symbols could be encoded with 7 binary bits, IBM decided in 1964 on a standard grouping of binary digits called the '**byte**'. The byte has eight bits, with the eight bit being a check bit.

Computer memory is arranged and addressed in bytes, and memory in computers is quoted in **Megabytes** (millions of bytes) or **Gigabytes** (thousands of millions of bytes).

When information (text, voice, pictures, video) is being sent over the Internet, the information is broken into blocks of bytes called '**packets**'[47].

The front 160 bits of each packet provides 12 pieces of information including how many bytes of data there are in the packet, where it came from and the address it is trying to get to.

---

[47] The concept of '*packet switching*' was first proposed by **Donald Davies** of the British National Physics Laboratory in 1964.

How does anti-virus software work?

Anti-virus software maintains a library of virus '*signatures*' in a database in your computer (or Smartphone or Tablet). A virus signature is a pattern of bits which is unique to a particular virus.

Your anti-virus software automatically scans every file coming into your computer looking for any of these signatures. Because the database may contain up to **60,000** signatures, this process will slow your computer down slightly, but it is a small price to pay for security.

It is estimated that hundreds of new viruses are released on the Internet ('*into the wild*') every day. While many or even most of these may not come your way, your computer must have the signatures in its database, just in case.

The anti-virus software suppliers have a laboratory where new viruses are examined and their signatures determined. All the anti-virus companies (with help from the CERTs[48]) cooperate and exchange information on viruses.

---

[48] **Computer Emergency Response Teams** (see more on these later)

The anti-virus suppliers send out updates almost every day with the newly detected virus signatures, so it is vital to download the updates every day if possible.

However, if a new virus spreads quickly before the companies detect it and send out the updates (a so-called '*day one'* **exploit**), there is nothing anyone can do – it may slip past the anti-virus protection and infect your computer.

Because of this, it is good practice to run your anti-virus software manually (an '*on demand'* run) through all your files about once a week to try and pick up these stray interlopers.

Security of Internet Transactions

Encryption – General

Financial transactions (shopping and banking) over the Internet are protected by scrambling the sent and received messages, so let us look at how this scrambling works.

When we were at school, we could write coded messages by substituting numbers for letters. The simplest scheme is '1' for 'A', '2' for 'B' and so on.

We could make the substitution a bit more difficult to unscramble by having a 'secret' key. For instance, if the secret key is '3' - meaning we add '3' to each number - then 'A' would be '4', 'B' could be '5' and so on.

We could obviously make the substitution scheme and the secret key a lot more complicated. The general term for the scrambling of messages is '*encryption*'.

To read the message, the receiver has to know what coding system is being used and the 'secret' key. This type of set-up is known as **'symmetrical encryption'**.

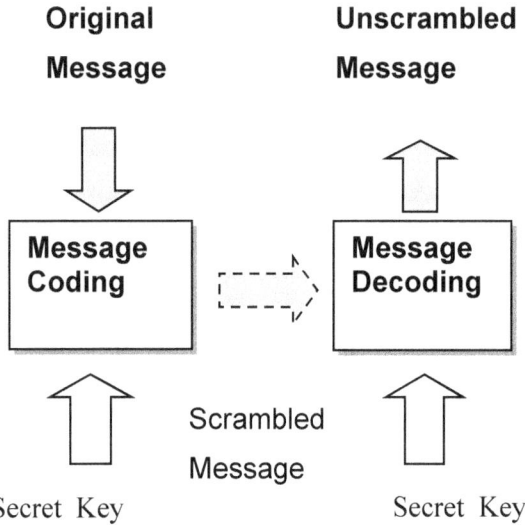

Letting the receiver know the coding system and the secret key in a secure way is relatively easy on a one-to-one basis. You could post the coding scheme in one letter and the secret key in another letter to the receiver.

Credit card firms do this when sending out your credit card – the card itself arrives in one envelope and the '*secret key*' (your PIN number) arrives in another. A further safeguard is that you generally must phone the credit card company to activate the card.

While this arrangement works for a small number of transactions or a small number of people, it becomes very difficult when millions of users are involved every day, as with on-line commerce. So a very important question for secure Internet transactions is: How do we securely exchange the 'secret' key?

A cunning scheme to solve this problem is **'Public Key Encryption'**.

How does Public Key Encryption work?

To recap: symmetrical encryption relies on a coding scheme (generally referred to as an *'encryption algorithm'*) and a *'secret'* key which are each known to both the sender and receiver of a message.

Public key encryption also relies on a coding scheme known to both sender and receiver, but instead of just a single shared 'secret' key, it uses **two** types of key:

- Each party (sender and receiver) has their own **'secret'** key known only to them; and

- Each party also has a **'public'** key, which is available to everyone.

The 'secret' and 'public' keys are generated as a **linked pair**. A message coded using a 'public' key can **only** be decoded using the matching 'secret' key. The reverse is also true – a message coded using a 'secret' key can **only** be decoded using the matching 'public' key.

Let us look at how this works in practice.

Alice wants to send a very sensitive message to Bob. She asks Bob to send her his 'public key' – say, attached to an e-mail.

Alice codes the message with Bob's 'public key' and sends the coded message to him, attached to an e-mail.

On receiving Alice's e-mail, Bob decodes the message using his 'secret' key, as only he can do.

Obviously it is important not to share your 'secret' key with anyone.

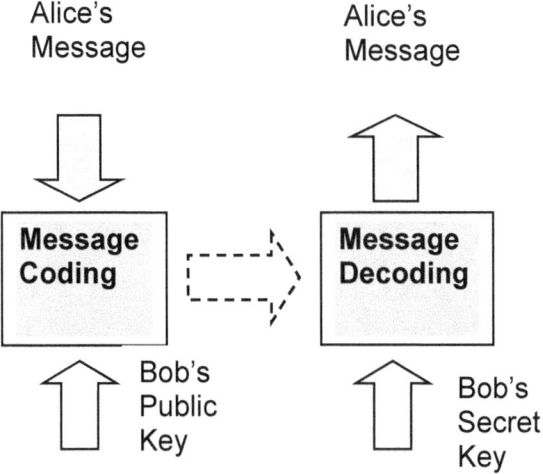

While the public key method described above works well, it is a bit slow, particularly if you are sending and receiving large amounts of data.

The usual practical set up is to use the faster symmetrical encryption for large amounts of data, and **securely exchange** the 'secret' key at the start of each session using Public Key Encryption[49].

---

[49] The 'secret' key in these cases is often referred to as a '**session**' key.

In our Internet banking and buying stuff, the good news is that all of this is set up automatically and we don't have to know how it works.

A good explanation of the concepts is given in *'The Code Book: The Secret History of Codes and Code Breaking'* written by Simon Singh[50].

---

[50] Also available as an e-book.

Who Invented Public Key Encryption

The basic concept of Public Key Encryption was developed by three people - **Hellman, Diffie** and **Merkle** at Stanford University in California over a few years up to 1975, but they could not come up with a workable system.

A practical implementation of the idea was devised by **Rivest**[51](right), **Shamir and Adelman** at MIT in Boston in 1977.

It was later revealed that two Englishmen, **James Ellis** and **Clifford Cocks**, had previously invented a practical system in 1973 at the UK Government GCHQ in Cheltenham, England, but it was kept secret.

---

[51] **Ron Rivest** actually thought of the solution one night when he could not sleep, but insisted on sharing the glory with his two co-researchers. The three friends founded the firm **RSA** - one of the most important Internet security providers. Ron is now a professor at MIT in Boston.

Security of Public Key Encryption

The Public Key Encryption uses mathematical entities called *'one-way functions'*[52]. These functions are relatively easy to calculate using computers, but reversing the process (that is, figuring out what the starting point was) is extremely difficult and time consuming, even with very fast computers.

The analogy sometimes used is making an omelette - fairly straightforward (for cooks). But reconstructing the eggs from the omelette is impossible.

Doing your own thing

If you want to securely exchange documents or data, a good starting point is to use free Public Key Encryption software called *'Pretty Good Privacy'* (PGP) written by **Phil Zimmermann**.

It takes a bit of learning and practice, but is worth the effort if you need confidentiality.

---

[52] The *'one-way functions'* are generally based on very large prime numbers and modulo exponentiation.

The 'secret key' is often two very large prime numbers and the 'public key' is the product of those two numbers.

All users will know (or be supplied with) the modulo number and the exponentiation (encoding) scheme.

Phil's Troubles

American Phil Zimmermann (below) released his PGP software package in 1991. The export of cryptographic systems with 'secret' keys longer than 40 digital bits was then forbidden as under US export regulations[53].

Since the PGP package used 128-bit keys, Phil was the subject of a criminal investigation when the PGP package was released ('*exported*') over the Internet.

The cunning Phil countered by publishing his software source code in a book. The legal precedent from two US Federal Appeals Court judgements was that published source code was protected under the First Amendment to the US Constitution (relating to free speech).

The investigation was closed without Zimmermann being charged.

---

[53] Security and law enforcement agencies were concerned that bad guys could use PGP to hide information or communicate with uncrackable messages.

What is SSL?

When we are using on-line banking or buying something over the Internet, we may see the acronym '*SSL*' appear (together with a small padlock symbol). SSL stands for **Secure Socket Layer**. So, what is a 'socket'.

When you are connected to the Internet, your PC (or laptop or tablet) is indentified by an **Internet Protocol (IP) address**, which is like an Internet phone number. It will look something like 211.15.108.32 - but we generally don't need to know what it is.

Because your computer is probably running a few applications (like e-mail and a web browser) at the same time and the incoming data packets are in a single stream, your computer needs to be able to work out where each packet of data should go.

This is achieved by allocating a unique '**port number**' to each application. For instance, e-mail is port 25 and browser traffic (like Internet Explorer or Chrome) is port number 80 or 8080[54]. The destination port number is included in each data packet you receive.

---

[54] For web proxy servers.

Your 'socket' is the **combination** of your IP address and the port number of the application you are using. The 'socket' therefore uniquely identifies your computer and the application you are using.

The *'layer'* bit refers to the Internet *'transport layer'* – the stream of data packets coming in and out of your computer.

Note: It is important to remember that the SSL security (that is, the data encryption) refers **only** to the data being exchanged between your computer and the institution you are dealing with. It **does not** secure the data on your computer or the data at the other end.

What is VoIP?

We have said that almost anything can be stored or transmitted in digital form. This is true of voice – on our mobile phone our voice is always sent and received as a digital stream.

VoIP is short for *'Voice over IP'*, where the IP refers to the Internet data transmission protocol (set of rules) called TCP/IP[55].

Many businesses and Government departments have moved over to VoIP desk phones[56].

With VoIP for home use, we typically use a conventional analogue phone plugged into a small box called a 'VoIP Gateway'. The gateway, which is connected to your computer network, converts voice into digital form and sends it to (and from) your chosen destination number.

---

[55] TCP/IP stands for **Transmission Control Protocol/Internet Protocol**.

[56] For example, see the desk phones on TV police dramas like *'New Tricks'* on ABC1-TV.

For VoIP, you need to have an arrangement with your Internet service provider – not all providers provide the VoIP service.
VoIP calls are generally much cheaper than conventional phone calls, particularly for overseas calls.

The downside of VoIP is that the quality is often not as good as conventional phones and if your computer stops, your VoIP stops too.

Skype

Skype is one of the most useful services on the Internet, particularly if you have family or friends a long way away.

Skype offers free computer-to-computer voice calls, provided both you and the person you are calling have installed the free Skype software (and also have a microphone and loudspeakers attached to each computer).

If both you and the person you are calling have a webcam, you can make video calls as well.

You can also make Skype calls from your Smartphone.

The question is – how does all this work and why is it free?

The reason it is free is that the users provide most of the infrastructure – your computer and your Internet connection is paid for by you.

Websites you look at are located on servers (provided by businesses or organisations) and your computer is the '*client*'. This type of set-up is called '*client – server*'.

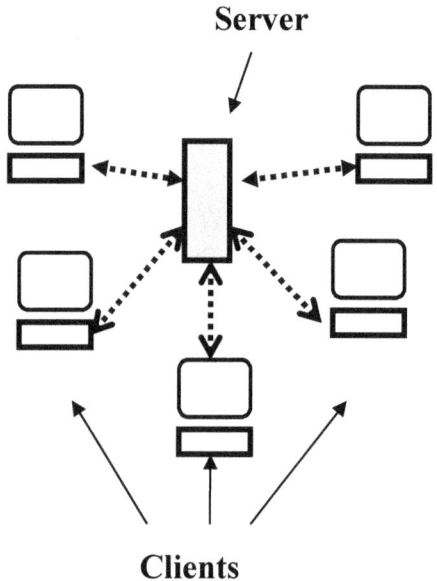

Server

Clients

Skype, on the other hand, does not have a central server. Messages pass directly from one computer (or Smartphone or Tablet) to another over the Internet – a so-called '*peer-to-peer*' arrangement.

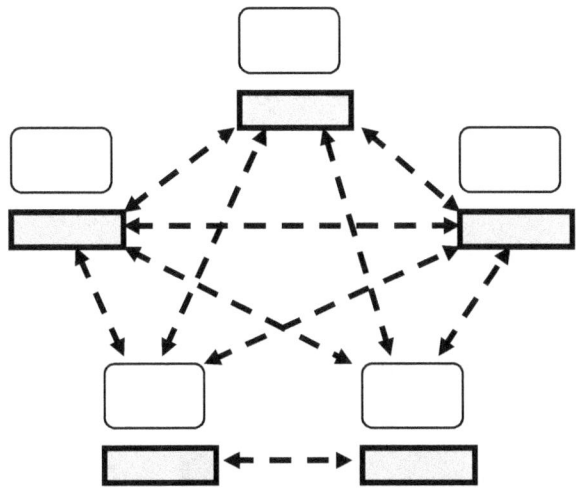

Peer to Peer

Skype makes its money from some advertising and from calls from your computer to mobile phones and ordinary landline phones for which it charges relatively low fees.

Voice and video calls between computers using Skype are believed to be encrypted with high grade encryption[57].

The original Skype software was written in Estonia. Skype is now owned by Microsoft.

---

[57] Skype does not say how, but key exchange is believed to use the **RSA** public key system and the symmetrical encryption is understood use the NSA-approved **Advanced Encryption Standard** (AES).

What is Wi-Fi?

Wi-Fi (pronounced '*Y Fye*') is the brand name of an international standard for wireless broadband access[58] within a small area like a home or office or cafe.

Wi-Fi is **not** the same as the wireless broadband networks (like 4G) for Smartphones, Tablets and laptops provided by the telephone companies, which cover a much larger area.

With Wi-Fi, a '**Wireless Router'**[59] transmits and receives the Internet data by radio to the surrounding area.

A Wi-Fi antenna in our PC, laptop or Tablet receives the transmitted data and converts it into a form our devices can understand. With outgoing data, the process is reversed.

---

[58] The standard is excitingly known as **IEEE 802.11**. The name Wi-Fi was devised by the brand consulting firm, **Interbrand**, alluding to the term Hi-Fi in audio equipment.

[59] Which often incorporates the ADSL modem which provides the connection to the Internet.

Wi-Fi is based on an invention by a team of Australian scientists and engineers, led by **John O'Sullivan** (on right) from the CSIRO[60] Radiophysics Division and derived from CSIRO's work in radio astronomy.

By 2012, the patents (after lengthy and expensive court cases against multinational technology companies) had yielded **$430 million** to CSIRO, with a lot more to come.

Most computers now have a Wi-Fi capability built in. This gives your device broadband Internet access when you are within range of a Wi-Fi 'hotspot' – a wireless network access point.

'Hotspots' are usually located at airports, shopping centres and coffee shops. Wi-Fi is usually a lot cheaper and faster that using your service provider's broadband wireless network.

---

[60] The (Australian) **Commonwealth Scientific and Industrial Research Organisation.**

When not within range of a Wi-Fi *'hotspot,* smartphones, tablets and laptops can turn to the wireless broadband to connect to the Internet.

A development being rolled out by some mobile phone companies for smartphones and laptops is **LTE** (Long-Term Evolution). This technology, marketed as '4G', is designed to provide very fast Internet connection speeds.

LTE uses some very fancy technology[61] and eventually aims to provide data speeds of up to **300 Megabits per second**.

An advantage of LTE for mobile phone operators is that quite a lot of the existing infrastructure can be used for the new LTE system.

---

[61] Such as **Orthogonal Frequency Division Multiple Access** (OFDMA), **Multiple Input – Multiple Output** (MIMO), **Spatial Division Multiple Access** (SDMA) and antenna beam forming. Try remembering this after a few drinks.

OFDMA is claimed to be very efficient in its use of the radio spectrum (delivering lots of data in a limited bandwidth).

More on CERTs

In the wake of the *'Morris Worm'*, the US Federal authorities decided that they had to do something to protect the Internet and its users.

The something was the establishment of a **Computer Emergency Response Team** (CERT) at the Carnegie-Mellon University in Pittsburg (right) in 1988.

The role of the team was to monitor the Internet for threats like viruses and worms and advise all stakeholders of the threats and help to work out what to do about it.

Over time, all developed countries set up their own CERTs and the US CERT took on the role of the world coordination centre (CC) for all the CERTs, so Pittsburg is now CERT-CC.

The CERT-CC role has expanded beyond the emergency response aspect to be more pro-active in improving security by:

- Helping countries to set up national CERTs;
- Conducting vulnerability analysis on software and systems;
- Developing methods and standards for secure software;
- Forensic analysis and cataloguing of malicious software; and
- Education in network and software security through the Carnegie-Mellon Software Engineering Institute.

The original Australian CERT (AusCERT) is based in the Prentice IT Centre at the University of Queensland in Brisbane. It issues warning and advisories and Internet users can register with their subscription service to receive bulletins.

In January 2010, the Australian Federal Government set up its own CERT, **CERT Australia**, also based in Brisbane.

CERT Australia is mainly focussed on working with critical infrastructure operators to protect Australia's important national interests.

Telecommunications

The Telegraph

The forerunner of the telephone was the telegraph, which made a huge impact on society at the time.

Australia's first telegraph line ran from Melbourne city to Williamstown from 1854.

Australia was connected to the early communications world in October 1872 when an undersea telegraph line was completed from Java to Darwin.

Darwin was the end point of a telegraph link to England via Singapore, India, Aden and Gibraltar.

In Australia, Darwin was the top end of the Overland telegraph line through Alice Springs to Adelaide, which in turn was linked to Melbourne.

An early telegraph story - with an Australian connection

John Tawell, who murdered his mistress and fled by train, was arrested following a telegraph message from Slough to Paddington Station on 1 January 1845.

This is believed to be the first use of the telegraph to catch a criminal (and the first use of a train to try and escape). Tawell was subsequently tried, convicted and hanged.

Tawell was convicted of forgery and transported to Australia in 1820. He obtained a '*ticket-of-leave*' and set up shop in Sydney as a chemist and did well. He served his sentence and returned to England a rich man around 1835.

In England he married a Quaker lady (his second wife) and settled down. He later took a mistress, Sarah Hart, but fearing that his affair would be discovered, he poisoned Sarah with prussic acid and then fled to London.

Alerted by the telegraph, the London police followed Tawell from the station and arrested him in a coffee shop.

The Telephone

Australia's first telephone service between the Melbourne and South Melbourne offices of Robinson Brothers began in 1879.

A public radio-telephone service between Australia and the UK was established by AWA in 1927.

The first undersea telephone cable linking Australia to the outside world (via Singapore and Hong Kong) was completed in 1967. The cable, which landed at Cairns, Queensland, was SEACOM[62] 2, with a capacity of **80** simultaneous two-way telephone calls[63].

Every continent (except Antarctica) is now connected to the international telephone system. It is said that the world telecommunications network is the largest system created by humans and is comparable in size and complexity to the human brain.

---

[62] SEACOM stood for **South East Asia Com**monwealth Telephone Cable. It was taken out of service in 1986.

The author worked in the ITT/STC Laboratory in London, England, where the SEACOM repeaters (amplifiers) were developed and manufactured.

[63] Present day **optic fibre** undersea cables can handle millions of simultaneous calls.

Without the world telecommunications network, the Internet as we know it today could not exist.

Where are we at now with telecomms?

The Australian telephone system has been evolving for over **130 years** and the vast majority of it is now digital. In the digital telephone world (which includes mobiles), there is no distinction between voice and data (which can be photos, video, music, whatever).

The exchanges (example on left) are all digital and the links between the exchanges are digital over optic fibre.

Many large buildings in the Central Business Districts of the capital cities are directly connected to optic fibre links for very fast voice and data transmission and reception.

Most intercontinental Internet traffic now goes by undersea optic fibre cable[64].

---

[64] While geostationary satellites are used extensively for television relays and some telecommunications, they can't handle the huge volume of data generated by the Internet.

The last area where the old ways are still in use is the connection between the exchanges and our homes and small businesses. Most of us are still connected to the exchanges by copper wires.

As we enter deeper into the Internet Age, our expectation of what is an acceptable Internet speed is rising rapidly. For example, from 2000 to 2010, there has been a **19,000%** increase in the volume of Internet downloads in Australia

While copper wires work well for voice and fax, they are very limited in the Internet speed they can deliver.

The nearest we can get to broadband with copper wires is with ADSL[65]. ADSL requires two '*boxes*' – an ADSL modem at your end and a DSLAM[66] card at the exchange.

---

[65] ADSL stands for **Asymmetric Digital Serial Line**. The asymmetric refers to the fact that it is much faster in one direction (the download to you) that the other (the uplink from you).

[66] DSLAM stands for Digital Serial Line Access Module.

ADSL shares a standard telephone line and does not interfere with calls because it sends and receives the data at much higher frequencies that the voice signals[67].

If you live right next to an exchange, the speed might be around **8 million bits per second** (Megabits per second or Mb/s), but the speed rapidly reduces with distance from the exchange[68].

---

[67] Sometimes referred to as *'out of band'* transmission.

[68] Users may also experience sharp reductions in speed if a large number of users are using the Internet at the same time and the data links to their exchange do not have sufficient capacity.

NBN

The original aim of the National Broadband Network (NBN) was to deliver an Internet download speed of **100 Mb/s** (and higher) to the majority of the Australian population[69] by laying high-speed fibre optic cables[70] directly to homes (and business).

The argument for high speed is that, as we become more Internet dependent in the future, the demand for high-speed data will increase rapidly. NBN Co. expected Internet download volumes to increase by **600%** by 2015.

NBN Co. anticipated that the high-speed links would have enabled video links to homes and GP's surgeries for medical and paramedical applications - likely to be very valuable with an ageing population

---

[69] The NBN aim was to connect **93%** of people in urban areas, with people in remote areas to be serviced by satellite and fixed wireless.

[70] See next section for a discussion of optic fibre cables.

One problem is that the technology for fibre to the home is evolving rapidly and decisions on adopting a particular technology now may cause problems in the future. In addition, the up-front cost of rolling out a national fibre to the premises system is very high.

> To achieve the coverage of most of Australia, NBN planned to roll out **200,000 kilometres** of the fibre optic cable.

Verizon FiOS System

An example of a large-scale optic fibre-to-the-home system is the US **Verizon FiOS** system which started in 2005. As of 2013, the system passes an estimated 18 million homes, with 5 million paying customers in 16 US States. The system provides '*bundled*' television, Internet and phone services to the home.

The standard installations give customers a choice of **15, 25** or **75 Megabits per second** (Mb/s) download speeds. In selected areas, download speeds up to **500 Mb/s** are available.

The Federal Coalition Government elected in September 2013 is reviewing the NBN Co plan with a view to reducing costs and speeding up the roll-out. It is likely to change the aim from *'fibre to the premises'* to *'fibre to the node'*, which means that the final few hundred metres to homes and businesses would be over copper rather than fibre. This arrangement would be fast, but not as fast as fibre all the way.

> A working example of *'fibre to the node'* (FTTN) technology is the **Transact** system in Canberra.

A problem with a national FTTN scheme is that an estimated 60,000 *'nodes'* would be needed to cover the whole country[71].

Maintaining that number of nodes could be expensive.

---

[71] Compared with an estimated 121 *'points of interconnect'* and lots of small buried street *'hubs'* for the *'fibre to the premises'* arrangement.

How does Optic Fibre Work?

Optic fibre consists of a very thin strand of glass - thinner than a human hair[72] - surrounded by a layer of protective cladding.

Cladding (Silicon Dioxide with Boron or Germanium additives)

Glass Fibre Core (Silicon Dioxide)

Cross-Section of Optic Fibre

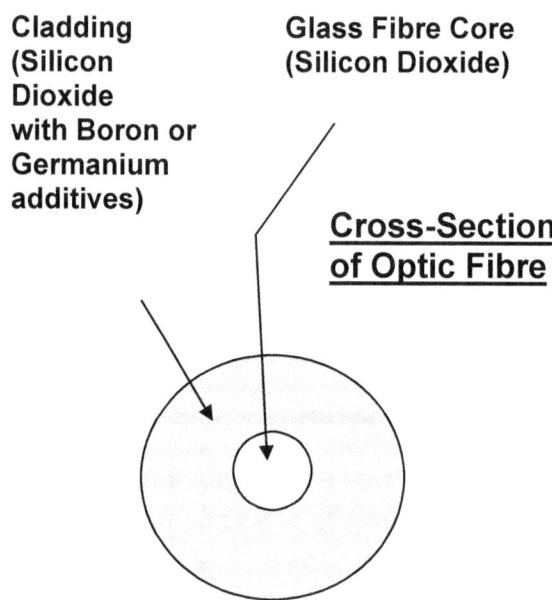

Boron Trioxide or Germanium Dioxide is added to the cladding to make its refractive index slightly different to the glass fibre core.

---

[72] A typical single-mode fibre core is about **8 micrometres** in diameter. Human hair diameter varies between about **17 and 180 micrometres**. A micrometer is a millionth of a metre.

Typical cladding is about **125 micrometres** in diameter.

The different in refractive index[73] allows the light pulses travelling along the core to bounce back off the core wall[74] (see the diagram below).

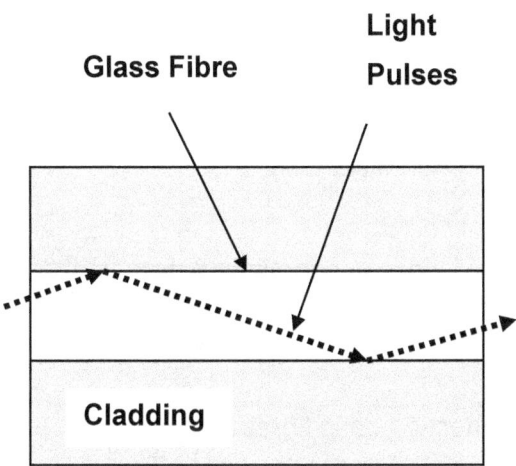

Side View of Optic Fibre

The Internet data is converted to laser light pulses which travel at the speed of light along the fibre core.

---

[73] A difference as small as **1%** is sufficient.

[74] A process known as '*total internal reflection*'. The fibre core acts as a **light waveguide**.

A typical optic fibre cable will have six or more fibres, with each fibre carrying data at about **40 Gigabits**[75] **per second**.

By using different laser light colours, each fibre can carry hundreds of times more data[76], but the technology to do this is quite expensive. It is often cheaper just to lay more fibre, particularly for short distances.

There are small losses as the light pulses travel along the fibre, so on long stretches amplifiers are inserted to restore the signal.

Note that connecting optic fibres is much harder than connecting copper wires. The ends of the fibres have to be cut and fused together using special equipment operated by people who know what they are doing.

There is an excellent visual demonstration of how an optic fibre works by **Professor Bill Hammack**[77] on YouTube. See EngineerGuy.com, Series 3.

---

[75] A **thousand million** bits per second

[76] A technology called **Wavelength-Division Multiplexing** (WDM).

[77] Bill teaches at the Chemical Engineering Department, University of Illinois at Urbana (in the US).

How did we end up with Personal Computers ?

The first real attempt at a programmable computer was a mechanical contraption devised in the 1820s by an Englishman, **Charles Babbage** (1791 – 1871). Charles never got his *'Analytic Engine'* to work[78], but in 1991 one of his later designs, the *'Difference Engine'*, was built and it did work. His original uncompleted unit is on display at the Science Museum in Kensington, London

Charles Babbage

While a student at Cambridge University, Babbage was a member of the Extractors Club, which was dedicated to getting members out of a madhouse should they be sent to one.

Babbage later became a Professor of Mathematics at Cambridge and invented the 'cow catcher' for steam locomotives.

---

[78] Possibly because it was designed to have **25,000 parts** and weigh **15 tonnes**.

Ada Lovelace

A supporter, assistant and friend of Babbage was Ada, Countess of Lovelace - the daughter of the poet, Lord Byron[79].

Although this is disputed, Ada is credited with being the 'first programmer' - of Babbage's machines. The US Department of Defence programming language 'Ada' is called after her[80].

The Countess was a keen gambler and tried to devise a mathematical system to win, which unfortunately failed dismally and landed her with big debts and a blackmail attempt. Luckily, hubbie William King, Earl of Lovelace, was loaded and bailed her out.

Sadly, Ada, who had three children, died of cancer aged 36.

---

[79] Lord Byron was famously described by Lady Caroline Lamb as *'Mad, bad and dangerous to know'*. Byron was killed in Greece fighting for Greek independence from the Ottoman Empire.

[80] The US military standard for the Ada computer language is MIL-STD-1815. Ada was born in 1815. Who said the military are not sentimental?

The Dawn of Electronics

Electronics as we know it today started with the invention of the amplifying valve[81] by **Lee De Forest** in the US in 1907.

The First Real Computer

In Germany, **Konrad Zuse** built the Z3, the world's first programmable, fully automatic computer.

On 12-MAY-1941 the electro-mechanical Z3 was demonstrated to scientists at the *Deutsche Versuchsanstalt für Luftfahrt*, (DVL)[82] in Berlin.

DVL used the Z3 to perform statistical analyses of wing flutter (a dangerous problem) in aircraft designs[83].

---

[81] Known in North America as *'vacuum tubes'*.

[82] The German Experimentation-Institution for Aviation.

[83] The original Z3 was destroyed in 1944 by the RAF urban renewal programme. You can see a fully functioning replica, built in the 1960s by the originator's company (Zuse KG) in the Deutsches Museum in Munich.

Code Breaking

The first programmable **electronic** computer was the '*Colossus*', built by a team led by **Tommy Flowers** at the British Post Office Research Station at Dollis Hill, London in 1943.

Colossus (above) was used at **Bletchley Park** in Buckinghamshire, England (known as '*Station X*') to break the German '*Enigma*' and '*Lorenz*' military codes[84].

Colossus and the code breaking was a closely guarded secret for many years after the war. It is credited by some people with shortening WWII by several years.

---

[84] See the 1986 play and later TV film '*Breaking the Code*' written by Hugh Whitemore. The play and film focus on the role of mathematician **Alan Turing** in cracking the German codes.

Post World War II

After World War II, large mainframe computers for business and government were the main focus in Europe and the US. These monsters filled large rooms and were programmed by a new breed of specialist mathematicians[85].

The Great Leap Forward

One of the major milestones in technology occurred in 1948. **Transistors** were invented by three American physicists Bardeen, Brattain and Shockley (below) working at the Bell Telephone Laboratories in New Jersey, USA[86].

Transistors quickly replaced electronic valves and cut the power consumption and size of electronics enormously.

The invention started an avalanche of new developments.

---

[85] In those days, programmers wore ties and tweed jackets with leather elbow patches. Many also smoked pipes for gravitas.

[86] For which they won the 1956 Nobel Prize for physics.

Computer and Memory Chips

The next step was to combine a complete transistor circuit in a single chip, first achieved by **Jack Kilby** of Texas Instruments in 1958.

The first complete computer in a chip is believed to have been developed in 1968 in the US for use in military aircraft, but was secret at the time.

The first commercially available computer on a single chip, the **Intel 4004**[87] was a released by the US Intel Corporation in 1971.

At this time, home computers were the preserve of geeks. Simple computers were made by from kits like the Altair 8800[88].

---

[87] Generally referred to as a '*microprocessor*'. Most domestic appliances (microwaves, dishwashers) now contain at least one microprocessor.

[88] In 1975 Harvard University drop-outs **Bill Gates** and **Paul Allen** formed **Microsoft** ('**micro**processor **soft**ware') to develop and sell BASIC programming language interpreters for the Altair 8800 micro-computer.

Personal Computing Arrives

Steve Jobs (the salesman, on left) sold his Volkswagen Microbus and **Steve Wozniak** (the larger technical guru and manufacturer, below) sold his HP calculator and both used the money to develop a home computer which could be used by non-specialists.

The very basic Apple 1 was unveiled in 1976.[89]

Money from Apple I sales allowed Wozniak to develop a much more sophisticated model, the Apple II – released in 1997 (right).

---

[89] An Apple 1 with full documentation sold at Christies Auctions in London in 2010 for **$US 210,000**.

The (IBM) Empire Strikes Back

The world's largest computer company (at the time) was IBM. It concentrated on computers for business, particularly large mainframes, and ignored the home market.

Eventually, growing sales of Apple IIs made IBM realise that the home market could not be ignored. IBM started a rush program to put together a competitor.

To speed up development, the IBM Personal Computer (PC) was made, as far as possible, from readily available parts[90].

In August 1981, IBM launched its new Personal Computer (PC) with the Microsoft MS-DOS operating system (see box below). Microsoft cleverly retained the rights to MS-DOS[91].

---

[90] Allowing the PC to be developed in 1 year instead of the usual 4 years for an IBM product.

[91] And provided the launch pad for the Microsoft squillions.

Bill & Paul's Lucky Break

IBM needed an operating system for its new PC and asked Bill Gates of Microsoft (on left) for advice. Gates recommended C/PM, the most popular operating system at the time[92]. C/PM was written by **Gary Kindall** of Digital Research.

When IBM went around to Kindall's house, he was out (flying his plane) and they had major problems dealing with his mum (who hated IBM).

Frustrated, IBM asked Microsoft to provide an operating system.

Microsoft (Paul Allen) had previously bought a non-exclusive licence to use another operating system, 86-DOS[93], from Seattle Computer Products.

In July 1981, Microsoft bought all rights to 86-DOS from Seattle Computer for $US50,000 (but did not reveal the IBM deal), and renamed it MS-DOS.

---

[92] With 600,000 copies sold.

[93] Originally called QDOS and written by Tim Paterson in 6 weeks, loosely based on C/PM.

The downside for IBM of making their PC from readily available parts was that it was much easier to copy than the Apple (which was mostly made from special Apple parts).

Reverse engineered copies of the IBM PC soon appeared and the home computer revolution was in full swing.

Paul Allen

Microsoft co-founder Paul Allen was diagnosed with Hodgkins Lymphoma in 1982. He was successfully treated with radiation therapy, but began to follow his own interests after he recovered.

Allen resigned as a director of Microsoft in 2000 and reportedly sold 68 million of his shares (he is said to still hold 138 million shares).

An investor and philanthropist, Allen is reputed to be the 48th richest man in the world.

How did the Internet happen?

Conception

After World War II, experimental psychologist **J C R ('Lick') Licklider** worked at Harvard University and later at the Massachusetts Institute of Technology (MIT) in Boston. He was interested in how the human ear and brain worked together to hear.

Because of their ability to analyse large amounts of data quickly, he came to see computers as having great potential as assistants to researchers and decision-makers.

Later, while a Vice-President of the consulting firm **Bolt, Beranek and Newman** (BBN) in Boston, Licklider fostered an interest in computers. This allowed BBN to become computer consultants who participated in the initial development of the Internet

In October 1962, Licklider was appointed director of the Information Processing Techniques Office (IPTO) at the US Department of **Defence Advanced Research Projects Agency** (DARPA).

While with DARPA, Licklider promoted the idea of a communications network connecting research computers which would allow scientists to share processing time, data and research papers.

In April 1963, in a series of memos to colleagues, Licklider outlined his proposal. He jokingly called it the *'Galactic Network'*. At DARPA, he was able to distribute seed funding which eventually led to the early Internet experiments.

The full flowering of Licklider's idea did not come until the advent of the World Wide Web[94] in the 1990s.

Labour Pains

The first experimental wide area network – a sort of primitive Internet – linked the Massachusetts Institute of Technology (MIT) in Boston to the University of Santa Monica in California using acoustic couplers and dedicated phone lines[95].

---

[94] Discussed a little later.

[95] Organised by **Tom Merril.**

The experiment proved that this approach would not work, but provided many useful lessons for the next stage.

The Birth of the Internet

With DARPA funding, the ARPANet remote computing network[96] began with four '*nodes*'[97]:

- University of California at Los Angeles (UCLA)[98];
- Stanford Research Institute (SRI), San Francisco;
- University of California, Santa Barbra (UCSB); and
- University of California, Santa Monica (UCSM).

The first connection (between UCLA and SRI) - at 50 kilobits per second - was made on **29-OCT-69**.

The first cross-US ARPANet connection was made between UCLA and BBN in Boston in 1970.

---

[96] Based on a plan drawn up by **Larry Roberts** at MIT, Boston.

[97] Connected computers.

[98] With Leonard Klleinrock, Vint Cerf, Steve Croker and Jon Postel.

In 1971, **Ray Tomlinson** at BBN developed the basic e-mail software and sent the first e-mail (using the '@' symbol).

Teething Problems

Different data transmission standards made interconnecting computers very difficult.

Bob Kahn and **Vint Cerf** (above) worked to solve this problem and in 1973 announced the development of a universal data transmission standard, the Transmission Control Protocol (**TCP**).

The ARPANet project was deemed to be completed and was formally wound up in 1978. The network itself continued in operation.

On January 1st, 1983 ARPANet, with 213 'hosts' (connected computers), formally adopted Kahn and Serf's **TCP/IP** transmission protocol suite. TCP/IP allows different types of networks to interact smoothly and in some people's view (particularly Vint Cerf's), marks the real 'Birth of the Internet'.

Adolescence

By the 1980s, ARPANet nodes were being added at the rate of one per month. The rapid expansion of the network started to make manual updating of host (computer) addresses impossible.

In 1983, **Paul Mockapetris** (on right) developed an automated address updating and look-up system called the **Domain Name System** (DNS) and recommended standardising addresses as 'user@host.domain'.

This was introduced to the network in 1984.

Adulthood

From the beginning of 1986 to the end of 1987, the number of connected networks grew from 2,000 to **30,000**. In 1987, the US National Science Foundation started to commercialise the Internet.

In 1989, on the other side of the Atlantic, Englishman **Tim Berners-Lee** (left) working at CERN[99], proposed the Hypertext Mark-Up Language (HTML) and the Hypertext Transport Protocol (HTTP) - the basic building blocks of the **World Wide Web** (WWW).

---

[99] C*onseil* E*uropéen pour la* R*echerche* N*ucléaire* – the world's largest particle physics laboratory near Geneva, Switzerland and the home of the Large Hadron Collider.

Australia Awakes to the Internet

In May, 1990, **Geoff Huston** and **Peter Elford** (at the ANU[100] in Canberra) set up **AARNet**, the first Australian Internet, for academics, researchers and students.

The first commercial Internet Service Provider (ISP) in Australia, connect.com.au Pty Ltd, was set up in 1992 by **Hugh Irvine**, **Joanne Davis** and **Ben Golding**.

The Web Arises

The World Wide Web kicked off in 1992.

Shortly afterwards, a Web browser called '**Mosaic**' was developed at the US National Centre for Supercomputing Applications (NCSA)[101] by a team led by **Marc Andreessen** and **Eric Bina**.

Mosaic was released free on the Internet in April 1993.

---

[100] The **Australian National University** in Canberra.

[101] Located at the University of Illinois at Urbana-Champaign.

Web Browsers

A web browser is an application program which can receive and display web content, including text, pictures and video. Special features, such as *'hypertext'* links to other pages, can be accessed with a mouse click.

In October 1994, a commercial web browser, **Netscape** was released.

In February 1994, two Stanford University Ph.D. students **David Filo** and **Jerry Yang** started listing web sites in a campus caravan. The list evolved into *'Yet Another Hierarchical Officious Oracle'* (**Yahoo**)[102].

By May 1995, **30,000** websites were in operation, doubling every two months.

In January 1996, another two Stanford Ph.D. students, **Larry Page** and **Sergey Brin** began research on a web search engine called *'BackRub'*. This leads to the incorporation of **Google** in September 1997.

---

[102] By 2006, Yahoo had 400 million users, with 3.4 billion page hits per day.

By 1997, there were over **1.5 million** websites in operation.

In 2000, **Jimmy Wales** (the moneybags) and **Larry Sanger** (the tech wizard) in the US started a free on-line encyclopaedia called **Wikipedia**. Wikipedia's articles are written collaboratively by volunteers around the world.[103]

Skype was developed in 2003 by entrepreneurs **Niklas Zennström, Janus Friis**, and a team of software developers based in Tallinn, Estonia. Skype is a software program that allows users to make voice, chat and video calls over the Internet to other Skype users free of charge.[104]

---

[103] By April 2008, Wikipedia was attracting **683 million** visitors annually, reading over 10 million articles in 253 languages.

[104] Skype was acquired by eBay in September 2005 for **$US 2.6 billion**. By April 2008, there were **12,547,006** concurrent Skype users online. Skype is now owned by Microsoft.

Who Runs the Internet?

The Internet is largely self-organising, but there are two important international bodies involved in the administration of the Internet and setting the technical standards:

ICANN

The *Internet Corporation for Assigned Names and Numbers* (ICANN), was set up to manage and coordinate the Domain Name System. The domain names are allocated through an ICANN subsidiary body, the **Internet Assigned Numbers Authority** (IANA).

ICANN is a non-profit private organisation which operates under the aegis of the US Department of Commerce.

The current Chair of the Board of Directors is **Steve Crocker**, (right) one of the founding fathers of the Internet[105].

---

[105] Steve drafted and sent out the first Request for Comment (RFC), the form of the technical standards for the Internet.

IETF

The technical rules for the Internet are set by another non-profit organisation, the **Internet Engineering Task Force** (IETF) which is organised by the Internet Society (ISOC).

The IETF is a volunteer body whose mission is:

> *"...to make the Internet work better by producing high quality, relevant technical documents that influence the way people design, use, and manage the Internet."*

Most of the volunteers are technical people from the technology industries and Internet Service Providers.

Anyone who can stand days of talks and discussions by and with geeks can attend IETF meetings, which are usually held in the US.

As a hangover from the early days of the Internet, the technical rules are still called Requests for Comment (RFC), with an identifying number.

Digital Natives and Immigrants

In his 2001 paper *'Digital Natives, Digital Immigrants'*[106], **Marc Prensky** focused on the impact on the US education system of a generation ('Gen Y' or 'Net Gen'), for whom computer technology was the norm.

Prensky asserted that:

> *'It is now clear that as a result of this ubiquitous* [digital] *environment and the sheer volume of their interaction with it, today's students think and process information fundamentally differently from their predecessors.*

and that:

> *'Our students have changed radically. Today's students are no longer the people our educational system was designed to teach.'*

---

[106] From *'On the Horizon'*, Marc Pransky, MCB University Press, Vol. 9 No. 5, October 2001.

As for the previous generation, Prensky wrote:

> 'Today's older folk were "socialized" differently from their kids, and are now in the process of learning a new language.
>
> As Digital Immigrants learn – like all immigrants, some better than others – to adapt to their environment, they always retain, to some degree, their "accent," that is, their foot in the past.
>
> There are hundreds of examples of the digital immigrant accent. They include printing out your email (or having your secretary print it out for you – an even "thicker" accent); needing to print out a document written on the computer in order to edit it (rather than just editing on the screen); and bringing people physically into your office to see an interesting web site (rather than just sending them the URL).'

However, detailed research in 2009 by **Barbara Combes** at Edith Cowan University (ECU) in Western Australia[107], suggests that at last some of Prensky's assertions may be wide of the mark.

As part of her Ph.D. thesis, in which she used the term *'Net Generation'* instead of *'Digital Natives'*, Combes conducted an (academic) **literature analysis;** a **web survey** (with 533 participants); **in-depth interviews** (with 40 participants); and gave two **information-seeking tasks** to the interviewees. All the participants were young adult students at ECU.

Combes' conclusion from her research is that:

'.....*members of the Net Generation may be tech-savvy, if by this we mean they are confident and disposed to use technology. [However] they are definitely not information literate.*

---

[107] Combes, B. (2009). *'Digital natives or digital refugees? Why we have failed Gen Y?'*; Proceedings of 38th Annual Conference of the International Association of School Librarianship, incorporating the 13th International Forum on Research in School Librarianship: *'Preparing pupils and students for the future, school libraries in the picture.'*; Albano Terme, Padova, Italy, IASL and the University of Padua.

They are unable to locate, authenticate, deconstruct (make meaning from) and use information effectively or efficiently from a range of electronic sources.

They are easily satisfied with the first piece of information they find, trust search engine results and exhibit a snatch and grab behaviour ('snaffling"), where there is little or no reading or interpretation of search results.

Members of the Net/Gen Y are teaching themselves how to use the Internet at a relatively young age (average 10 years of age) which has led to the development of an entrenched culture of use that is based on simple search techniques and Google.

Thus, the idea of a generation of super users who can find information easily on the internet is not a reality.

They are also extremely confident, which means breaking their culture of use is going to be difficult and must occur at a young age.

The results of this research study indicate that a generation of young people who are digital natives is a perception rather than a reality. Schools have already failed the Net/Generation Y, since they have not provided in-depth teaching on how to develop the skills necessary to use electronic resources and the Internet when seeking information.'

Combes is concerned because:

'*...there has been a concerted effort on the part of governments in Australia and the rest of the world to cut costs by placing everything online as a means of providing "open and transparent government" and immediate access to service provision for citizens*'; and thus

'*...being able to navigate the new information landscape is becoming increasingly important for our citizens of tomorrow.*'; because

'*...it is assumed* [by Governments] *that the next generation will require [information to be] only online, since [citizens will] already have the skills necessary ....to find information.*'

and she thinks the following quotation is now more relevant than ever:

> 'Information seeking must be one of our most fundamental methods for coping with our environment. The strategies we learn to use in gathering information may turn out to be far more important in the long run than specific pieces of knowledge we may pick up in our formal education and then soon forget as we go about wrestling with our day-to-day problems.' (Donohew, Tipton & Harvey, 1978).

Combes recommends:

> 'Using the Internet for information seeking and developing information literacy skills needs to be embedded in curriculum programs in the early primary school years if educators are going to impose a different culture of use on this generation of users.'

Gen X might be a bit slower on the Internet, but to compensate, they do have a wealth of life experience and generally a mature, responsible and measured approach to gathering and using information.

The Psychology of Scams

The UK OFT Report

The United Kingdom Office of Fair Trading (OFT) found that **3.2 million** adults are victims of scams every year in the UK. The losses by victims were estimated to be **3.5 billion pounds**.

In an effort to find out more about the problem, OFT asked the Department of Psychology at Exeter University to prepare a report on scamming and the victim's decision-making.

Scam Features

The OFT report[108] found that:

> "A successful scam involves all the standard elements of the 'marketing mix' and the building of a relationship between marketer and customer– that is, between scammer and victim."

---

[108] 'The Psychology of Scams: Provoking and Committing errors of Judgement', Prepared for the Office of Fair Trading by the University of Exeter School of Psychology, May 2009

and that:

> "...the way in which they are marketed has much in common with legitimate products."

The researchers found "....similarities between scams in their content and the use of persuasive techniques", with two techniques being the most common:

> • "**appeals to trust and authority**: [the scammers used] ....cues that make the offer look like a legitimate one being made by a reliable official institution or established reputable business;" and

> • "**visceral triggers:** scams exploit basic human desires and needs – such as greed, fear, avoidance of physical pain, or the desire to be liked –in order to provoke intuitive reactions and reduce the motivation of people to process the content of the scam message deeply. For example, scammers use triggers that make potential victims focus on the huge prizes or benefits on offer."

The report noted that scammers used a number of techniques to reel their victims:

- "Scams are often **personalised** to create the impression that the offer is unique to the recipient."

- "They also emphasise the **urgency** of a response to reduce the potential victim's motivation to process the scam content objectively"

- "Scammers ask their potential victims to make **small steps** of compliance to draw them in, and thereby cause victims to feel committed to continue sending money"

- "The disproportionate relation between the size of the alleged reward and the cost of trying to obtain it. Scam victims are led to focus on the alleged big prize or reward in comparison to the relatively small amount of money they have to send ...to obtain their windfall, a phenomenon called **'phantom fixation'**."

The Victims

The report noted that, while responding to a scam was clearly an error of judgement, the victims, in general, were **not** poor decision-makers.

The research suggested that victims are often acting against their own better judgement - with some part of their minds they recognise a scam for what it is. The researchers suggested that any awareness raising campaigns should emphasise that, if you think an offer might be a scam, it almost certainly is – your gut instinct is almost invariably right.

Compared to non-victims, scam victims report being less able to regulate and resist **emotions** associated with scam offers. They seem to be unduly open to persuasion, or perhaps unduly undiscriminating about who they allow to persuade them.

This creates an extra vulnerability in those who are socially isolated, because social networks often induce us to regulate our emotions when we otherwise might not.

For example, it was striking how some scam victims kept their decision to respond private and avoided speaking about it with family members or friends. It was almost as if with some part of their minds, they knew that what they were doing was unwise, and they feared the confirmation of that. Indeed to some extent they even hide their response to the scam from their more rational selves.

Background Knowledge

Another counter-intuitive finding is that scam victims often have better than average background knowledge in the area of the scam content.

For example, it seems that people with experience with legitimate prize draws and lotteries are more likely to fall for a scam in this area than people with less knowledge and experience in this field.

This also applies to those with some knowledge of investments. Such knowledge can increase rather than decrease the risk of becoming a victim.

Analysing Scam Content

The researchers did not expect to find that scam victims put more effort into analysing scam content than non-victims. This contradicts the intuitive suggestion that people fall victim to scams because they invest too little time or energy investigating their content, and thus overlook information that might betray the scam.

This may, however, reflect the victim being 'drawn in' to the scam while non-victims include many people who discard scams without giving them a second glance.

From the victim interviews it was clear that some people viewed responding to a scam as taking a long-odds gamble: they recognized that there was something wrong with the offer, but the size of the possible prize or reward (relative to the initial outlay) induced them to give it a try on the off-chance that it might be genuine.

Vulnerability

The research suggests that there is a minority of people who are particularly vulnerable to scams. In particular, people who reported having previously responded to a scam were consistently more likely to show interest in responding again. Though a minority, it is not a small minority; depending on how it is assessed, it could be between **10 and 20 per cent** of the population.

The existence of individual differences in how persuadable people are throws some light on the fact that some people become 'chronic' or serial scam victims: it would not be surprising to find that such victims are exceptionally **highly persuadable** – though that is unlikely to be the complete explanation of chronic victimhood, as other factors such as cognitive impairment may be involved.

The WA Government on Scams

The Western Australia Department of Commerce has a good website at www.scamnet.wa.gov.au.

The website lists some of the tricks that scammers use:

Reciprocation

Scammers give you something, such as a 'free' gift or assistance, to get something in return, such as your agreement later on. You are caught up feeling obliged to do something.

Commitment and consistency

Someone will get you to commit to something early in the piece, and later recall that initial agreement to get you to agree to something further. This ploy can make you feel ill at ease.

Social proof

'Everybody does it, so it must be right' pretty well sums it up. The other person will refer to what the majority does to get you to agree.

Liking

Good looks, similar interests or background, humour and other attractive characteristics are standard tools for the con-artist as well as of course for honest people who want to generate good rapport with you. If you like someone, you're more likely to go along with what they are suggesting.

Authority

Authority, in or out of uniform, will cause an automatic response in almost everyone. We appeal to and use authority all the time to justify or support our position. Scammers do it deliberately to hoodwink you into agreement.

Scarcity

The fear of missing out! Being told that this is the last chance or that there are only so few still available, leads most people to agree hastily before they have had the opportunity to think about what they're doing. Some people have found themselves in horrible financial situations because they rushed into agreements or purchases in the fear of missing out.

Personalised scams

Personalised scams occur when a scammer gathers your personal information and uses it to specifically target you with a scam. The fact that the scammer knows so much about you may lead you to believe they are legitimate.

ACCC Video

The WA Department of Commerce website also has a short video by the Deputy Chairman of the Australian Competition and Consumer Commission (ACCC) **Peter Kell**, which discusses some specific examples of personalised scams and how you can avoid them.

Much of the material on the WA website is based on the book '*Influence: The Psychology of Persuasion*', by Robert Cialdini (ISBN 0688128165).

Data Formats

Files on your computer have a general form: *'filename.extension'*.

An example would be 'Minutes18DEC12.doc' if you were typing up the minutes of the Begonia Society committee meeting using the Microsoft Word application

The filename should hopefully tell you something about the contents, while the extension (the .doc part) tells you which application was used to create the file.

Listed below are some extension examples and suggestions of how to read the files:

Extension	Application	To Read
.doc	Microsoft Word (early version)	Microsoft Word or Open Office (free download)
.docx	Microsoft Word (later versions)	As above
.pdf	Portable document format	Adobe Acrobat (free download)
.jpg, .tiff	Photo	Microsoft Windows Media Player or Photoshop
.htm	Web document	Any web browser
.wav	Audio	Microsoft Wave

Extension	Application	Notes
.exe	Executable program	Any operating system.
.zip	Compressed file	Any zip software.
.xls	Excel file	Microsoft Excel
.mp3	Compressed audio	MP3 player
.htm, .html	Web page	Any web browser.
.mwv	Compressed video	Windows Media Player.

'Staysmartonline' Factsheets

These Factsheets are available at:

http://www.staysmartonline.gov.au/factsheets

Factsheet 1 - Secure computing checklist

Factsheet 2 - Setting up automatic updates in Windows XP

Factsheet 3 - Setting up a limited user account in Windows XP

Factsheet 4 - How to secure Outlook Express in Windows XP

Factsheet 5 - How to secure Mozilla Thunderbird

Factsheet 6 - Securing the Microsoft Internet Explorer 9 web browser

Factsheet 7 - How to secure Windows Live Mail

Factsheet 8 - Securing the Mozilla Firefox web browser

Factsheet 9 - What is a web site digital certificate and why is it important to check?

Factsheet 10 - How to detect phishing sites and steps to prevent being fooled by them

Factsheet 11, Part 1 - You suspect your computer is infected with malicious software - what should I do?

Factsheet 11, Part 2 - You suspect your computer is infected with malicious software - what should I do?

Factsheet 11, Part 3 - You suspect your computer is infected with malicious software - what should I do?

Factsheet 12 - How to create back-up copies of your important information

Factsheet 13 - Understanding and reducing security risks associated with peer to peer file sharing

Factsheet 14 - Issues to consider before formatting your hard disk and when it is recommended

Factsheet 15 - Understanding password security

Factsheet 16 - Securely configuring your broadbandmodem/router

Factsheet 17 - Wireless (Wi-Fi) security

Factsheet 18 - Free security software (Microsoft Windows XP and Microsoft Windows Vista)

Factsheet 19 - Social engineering: what is it and how it can be used for fraudulent purposes

Factsheet 20 - Web threats: what are they and what you can do to protect your computer and information?

Factsheet 21 - Choosing an alternative browser

Factsheet 22 - Setting up automatic updates for Windows Vista

Factsheet 23 - Setting up automatic updates for Windows 7

Factsheet 24 - Setting up automatic updates for Apple Mac OS X

Factsheet 25 - Using Apple Software Update on Microsoft Windows

Factsheet 26 - Stay Smart Online - Raising Awareness on Cyber Security

Factsheet 27 - Stay Smart Online Alert Service

Factsheet 28 - Setting up a standard user account in Windows 7

User Guide

www.ingramcontent.com/pod-product-compliance
Lightning Source LLC
Chambersburg PA
CBHW060857170526
45158CB00001B/394